Disney
Kids Readers

Workbook and **eBook**

Level
2

Sandy Zerva

P Pearson

Disney

Kids Readers

Workbook · eBook

Level
2

Sandy Zerva

Contents

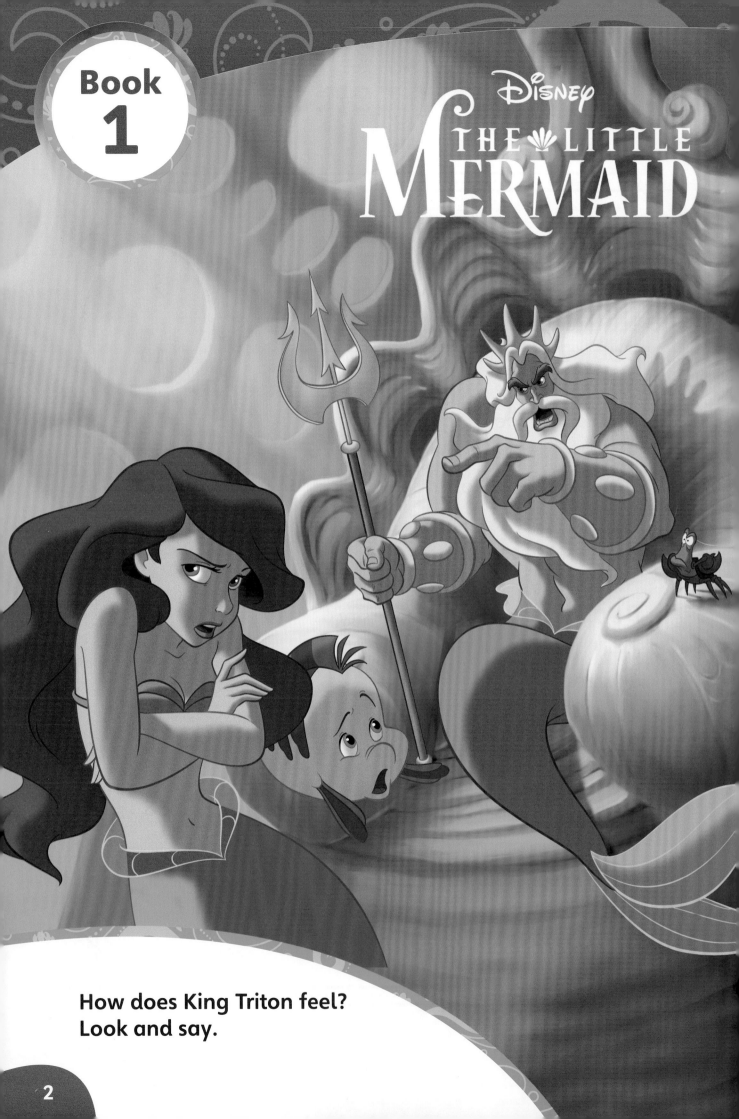

Book 1

Disney

THE LITTLE
MERMAID

How does King Triton feel?
Look and say.

Vocabulary

1 **Find the words.**

| beach   love   fall   human   ~~mermaid~~   swim |

demer(mermaid)allinlovhugersohumanlovieandem
orbeachormedswimmerfaleloveinfallmaidonbat

2 **Look and circle.**

1

swim / fall

fork / ship

2

cloud / storm

mermaid / human

3 **Write. Use words from Activities 1 and 2.**

1 Fish and mermaids can _____ .

2 They're on the _____ .

3 Ariel is a _____ now.

4 There's a _____ .

Story

1 Match the words (a–f) to the sentences (1–6).

a Prince Eric

b the water

c her father

d human things

e the beach

f Ariel

1 Ariel loves ....

2 Prince Eric falls in ....

3 Ariel takes Prince Eric to ....

4 Ariel sings about ....

5 King Triton is angry with ....

6 Ariel leaves ....

2 Look at the scenes. How does Ariel feel? How do you feel? Write.

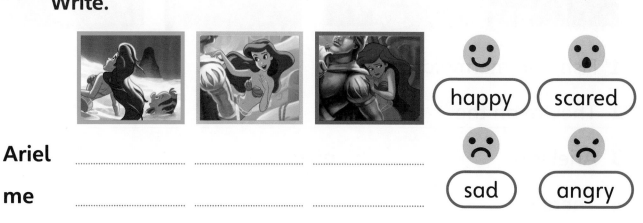

Ariel ....

me ....

happy   scared

sad   angry

Language

1 🎧 **Listen and read.**

💬 **Language**

Whose bag is **this**?   **Whose** glasses are **these**?
It's **my** bag.   They're **Kai's** glasses.
[It's = It **is**   They're = They **are**]

---

2 **Look, read, and write.**

Nick

Mia

1 Anna: _____ dog
             is this?

   Paul: It's _____ dog.

2 Chris: _____ shoes are these?

   Mia: They're _____ shoes.

3 Tom: Whose watch _____ _____ ?

   Ellie: It's _____ watch.

4 Alex: _____ books _____ _____ ?

   Liv: _____ books.

3 **Practice the dialog. Use these words.**

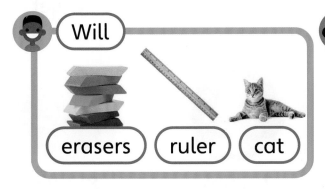

Will

erasers   ruler   cat

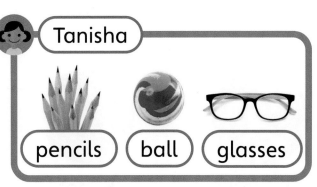

Tanisha

pencils   ball   glasses

Phonics

1 🎧 **Listen and circle. Which sound do you hear, e or i?**

1
e
i

2
e
i

3
e
i

4
e
i

5
e
i

6
e
i

2 🎧 **Listen and write e or i.**

T___n b___g f___sh and s___x r___d f___sh

Sw___m quietly.

They don't have l___gs.

To walk, you see.

3 🎧 **Read. Match the rhyming words. Listen and check.**

1 drink   **2** red   **3** Tim   **4** get

5 bed   **6** pet   **7** think   **8** swim

Values: Courage

1 **What is Ariel's dream? Check.**

To meet Prince Eric

To walk

2 **What is your dream? Draw and write.**

I want to ....

3 **Share.**

I want to fly a plane.

Find Out

1 **Read and circle.**

1 In a storm, you can see **clouds / the sun**.

2 In a storm, you can hear **lightning / thunder**.

3 In a storm, **go under a tree / move away from trees**.

4 In the house, **move away from / stand next to** the window.

Writing tip

It's windy today! ←

Use exclamation marks to show excitement and surprise.

2 **Read. Add an exclamation mark or a question mark.**

1 Look at the lightning. It's scary......

2 Listen to the thunder. It's loud......

3 I can hear the rain. Is it heavy......

4 We can't go out. The wind is very strong......

5 Can you see that dark cloud......

6 Look at the snow. It's beautiful......

Game Follow the Path

Start

1 Spell it.

p _ n c i l

2 How many legs?

3 Yes or No?

It's a storm.

4 Say it.

What is your dream?
I want to _____.

6 Spell it.

s _ h _ p

5 Whose dog is it?

This is _____ dog!

7 Say it.

_____ are
my books.

8 Say it.

Humans walk.
Mermaids _____.

9 Human or mermaid?

10 Say it.

These _____ are
dark.

Finish

Now I can ...

◯ understand and use key words from the story.

◯ ask and answer questions about people's things.

◯ hear the difference between sounds for e and i and say them.

Disney · PIXAR
FINDING DORY

What animals can you see?
Look and say.

Vocabulary

1 Read and color.

octopus =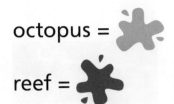

reef =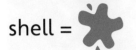

shell =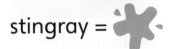

stingray =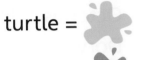

turtle =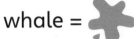

whale =

1
2
3
4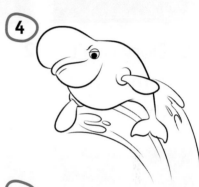
5
6

2 Draw lines to match.

(far)   (path)   (forget)   (remember)   (tank)

1
2
3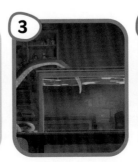
4
5

Story

1 Look and read. Match the sentences 1–4 to the sentences a–d.

1 Dory can't remember the way. ....

2 Dory meets Marlin and Nemo. ....

3 Dory hits her head. ....

4 Hank the Octopus helps Dory. ....

a She remembers!

b She can't go home.

c She finds her parents.

d She goes to school and has friends.

2 Draw and label your favorite character from the story.

This ....

Language

1 🎧 **Listen and read.**

> 💬 **Language**
>
> What **are** you do**ing**?   What**'s** she do**ing**?
> I**'m** writ**ing**.   She**'s** listen**ing** to music.
> We**'re** play**ing** a game.
> [We**'re** = We **are**   She**'s** = She **is**   What**'s** = What **is**]

2 **Read and write.**

1 Sophia: Hi Ryan. What _____
                    you doing?

2 Ryan: I _____ _____ **(draw)** a picture.

3 Sophia: What's Harry _____ ?

4 Ryan: He _____ _____ **(write)** a story.
                    What _____ you and your sister
                    _____ ?

5 Sophia: We _____ _____ **(watch)** TV.

3 **Practice the dialog. Use these words and your own.**

help mom

make a cake

wash my hands

wait for the bus

Phonics

1 🎧 Help Dory go home. Listen and circle j or wh.

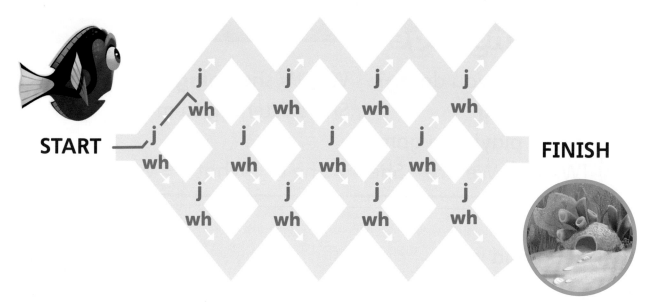

START — FINISH

j / wh

2 🎧 Listen and write J, j, Wh, or wh.

"......ere is Dory?"

Says ......enny to the ......ale.

"......ump on my tail,"

Says the big, ...ite ......ale.

3 🎧 Read and match. Listen and check.

(juice)　(white)　(jeans)　(where)　(wheel)　(jug)

Values: Determination

1 **Read and circle a or b.**

Dory wants to go home, but it isn't easy. What does she do?

a She stops trying.

b She keeps trying.

2 **Read, and check (✔) or cross (✗). Then add one more thing.**

I try again and again. ◯

I ask for help. ◯

When something is difficult …

I don't want to do it. I stop. ◯

I get angry. ◯

I talk about it. ◯

_____ ◯

3 **Share.**

I'm learning to roller skate.
It's difficult. My dad is helping me.

Find Out

1 **Read and answer Yes or No.**

1 Octopuses can swim fast. ....

2 All octopuses are dangerous. ....

3 Octopuses can hide very well. ....

4 Some octopuses squirt ink to catch animals. ....

Writing tip

She's on the reef.

They're fast.

Use contractions in everyday speaking and writing.

2 **Write. Use contractions.**

1 Octopuses are smart.

They're smart.

2 Octopuses' arms are strong.

They ....

3 The Pygmy octopus is very small.

It ....

4 Blue whales are very big.

They ....

5 The stingray is dangerous.

It ....

6 Dory is a Pacific blue tang fish.

She ....

Game   Spin the Wheel

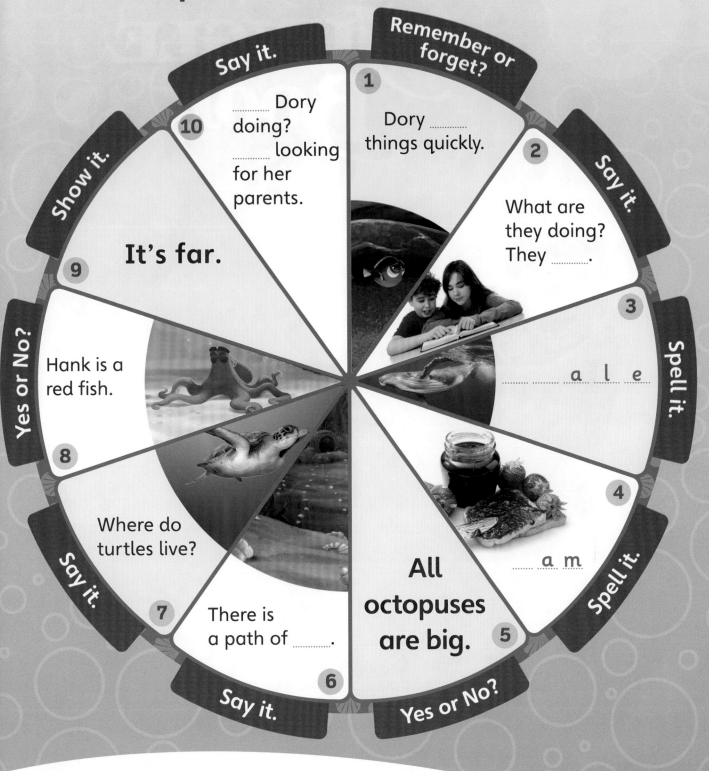

Say it. — Remember or forget?

1. Dory _____ things quickly.

10. _____ Dory doing? _____ looking for her parents.

Say it. 2. What are they doing? They _____.

9. It's far. **Show it.**

Spell it. 3. _____ a l e

8. Hank is a red fish. **Yes or No?**

Spell it. 4. _____ a m

7. There is a path of _____. **Say it.**

Say it. 6.

5. All octopuses are big. **Yes or No?**

Where do turtles live?

Now I can...

◯ name things and animals in the ocean.

◯ ask and say what people are doing at the moment.

◯ hear the difference between sounds for j and wh and say them.

17

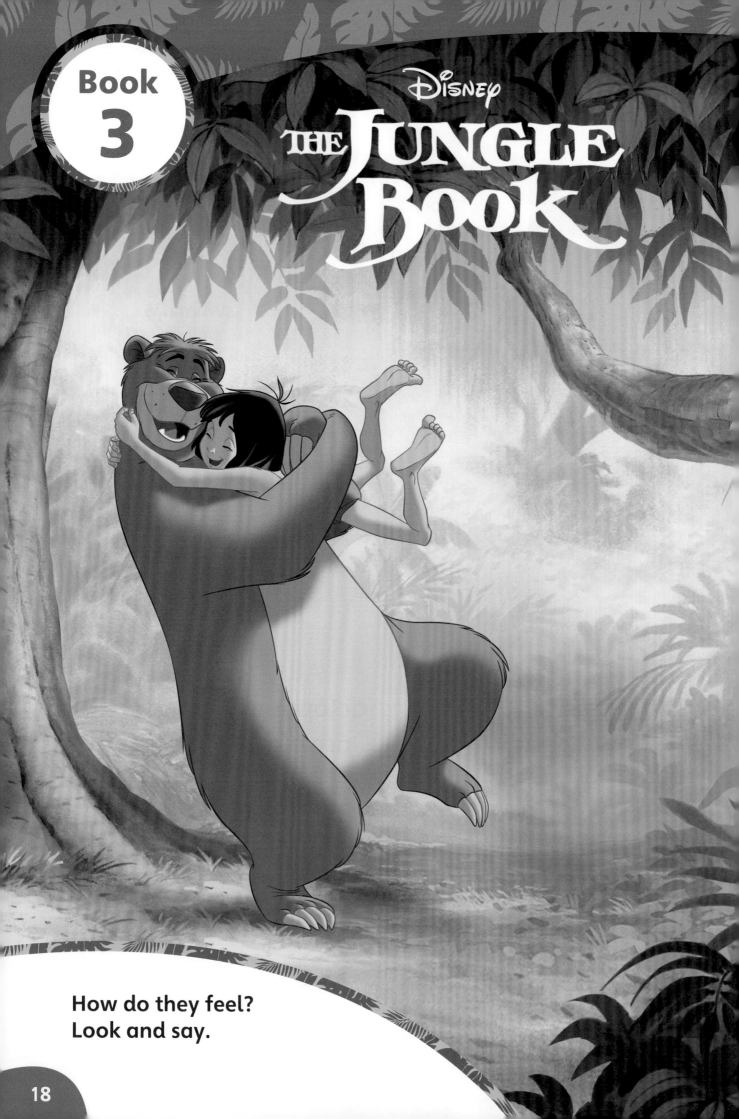

Book 3

Disney

THE JUNGLE BOOK

How do they feel?
Look and say.

Vocabulary

1 **Read, find, and write.**

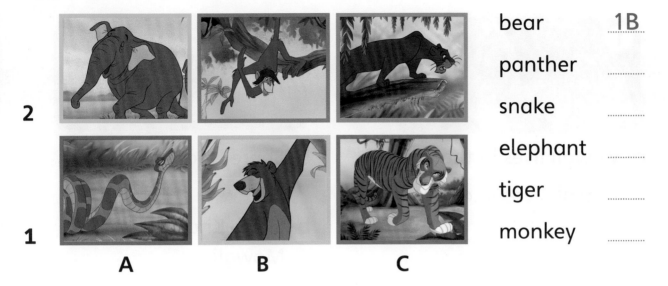

bear	1B
panther	....
snake	....
elephant	....
tiger	....
monkey	....

2 **Do the crossword.**

> dangerous   friendly   have fun   jungle   river   together

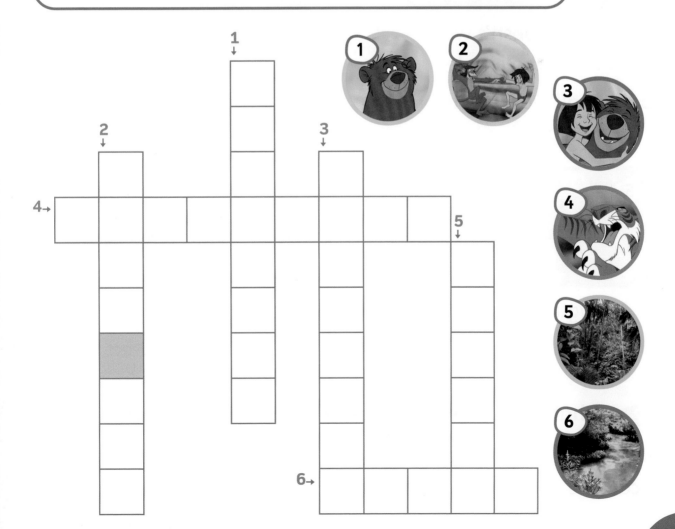

Story

1 **Read and circle.**

a Mowgli lives in the jungle.

b Mowgli lives in a town.

a Shere Khan is Mowgli's friend.

b Shere Khan doesn't like Mowgli.

a Mowgli doesn't want to leave the jungle.

b Mowgli wants to leave the jungle.

a Baloo is a friendly bear.

b Baloo is a dangerous bear.

a Mowgli wants to help Baloo.

b Baloo wants to help Mowgli.

a Baloo isn't happy.

b Mowgli isn't scared now!

2 **What is your favorite scene? What can you see?**

My favorite scene is on page _____. In this scene,
I can see _____.

20

Language

1 🎧 **Listen and read.**

> ## 💬 Language
>
> | | |
> |---|---|
> | What **do** you **do** on the weekend? | We **play** computer games. I **go** to the park. |

2 **Choose and write.**

(have   do   see)

1 🧑 Maria: What do you do on the weekend?

👧 Kat: I _____ my friends. We _____ things

together. We _____ fun.

(buy   do   eat   go   do)

2 😀 Bill: What _____ you _____ on the

weekend?

👦 Louis: We _____ to the mall. We _____

books and we _____ ice cream.

3 **Practice the dialog. Use these words and your own.**

watch TV

play in the yard

go to the movies

visit my grandmother

21

Phonics

1 🎧 **Listen and check.**

1 bug ⭕
bag ⭕

2 cut ⭕
cat ⭕

3 hat ⭕
hot ⭕

4 run ⭕
Ron ⭕

5 not ⭕
nut ⭕

6 Pat ⭕
pot ⭕

2 🎧 **Listen and write a, o, or u.**

The j____ngle is h____t. The river is n____t.

A panther is a c____t. It doesn't have a h____t.

It r____ns and j____mps. It does n____t st____p.

3 🎧 **Read the words in Activity 1. Put them in the correct list. Listen and check.**

a as in *cat*   **u** as in *bug*   **o** as in *hot*

....

....

....

Values: Friendship

1 **Who helps Mowgli? Check. Then write.**

 Kaa ○

 Shere Khan ○

 Baloo ○

 King Louie ○

_____ helps Mowgli. He is his friend.

2 **Do the friendship quiz. Read and check. Count your score.**

○ I remember my friend's birthday.

○ I share my things with my friend.

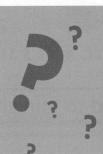

○ I make my friend laugh.

○ I say "I'm sorry" to my friend when I'm wrong.

○ I help my friend.

○ I don't say bad things about my friend.

Results:
5–6 😃 You're a great friend!
3–4 🙂 You're a good friend.
1–2 😲 Please go to Friendship School! 🙂

3 **Share.**

 I share my snacks with my friend.

Find Out

1 **Choose and write.**

In the rainforest, …

> trees important hot mangoes

1 it is _____ and sunny.

2 there are very tall _____.

3 you can find coconuts, bananas and _____.

4 there are _____ plants and animals.

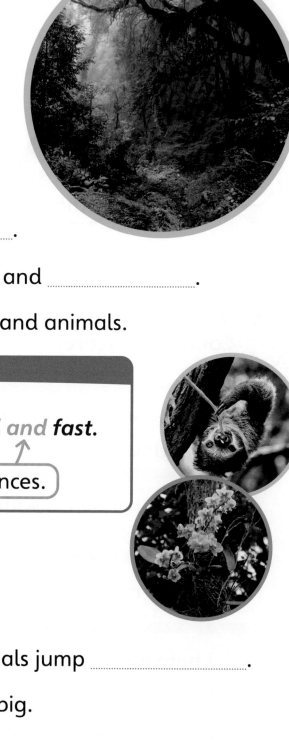

Writing tip

*It's small. It's fast. = It's small **and** fast.*

Use **and** to join sentences.

2 **Join the sentences. Use *and*.**

This is the rainforest.

1 Animals jump. Animals fly. Animals jump _____.

2 The trees are tall. The trees are big.

The trees are _____.

3 Monkeys eat fruits. Monkeys eat flowers.

Monkeys _____.

4 Flowers are beautiful. Flowers are colorful.

_____

Game   Connect Three in a Line

1 Spell it.

j _ _ n g l e

2 Say it.

Mowgli and the monkey have ....

3 What's the word?

v r i r e

4 Yes or No?

Mowgli is scared.

5 Say it.

What .... on the weekend?
We go to the beach.

6 Spell it.

_ p _ l _ _ n t

7 Yes or No?

It is cold in the rainforest.

8 Friendly or dangerous?

9 Who helps Mowgli?

.... Mowgli.
They are ....

Now I can ...

◯ name and describe things and animals in the jungle.

◯ ask and say what I do on the weekend.

◯ hear the difference between sounds for a, u, and o, and say them.

Book **4**

Disney · PIXAR

TOY STORY

Where are Andy's toys? What are they looking at? Look and say.

Vocabulary

1 **Draw lines to match.**

presents   plane   badge

laugh   wing   birthday party

a   **b**   **c**

d   **e**   **f**

2 **Look and read. Then check or cross.**

1 fly ◯   **2** laugh ◯   **3** fast ◯   **4** smart ◯

3 **Choose, draw, and write. Make words from Activities 1 and 2.**

1 pl ane

2 w

3 pre

4 ba

5 sm

6 la

ing   dge   ane   art   ugh   sent

Story

1 **Put the story in the correct order.**

1 d

2 Today is Andy's party.

3 ....

4 Woody doesn't like Buzz.

5 ....

6 Look at Buzz! He's smart and fast!

7 ....

8 Woody and Buzz are friends now.

a Andy gets a new toy. His name is Buzz.

b Buzz jumps on a ball. It helps him fly!

c Woody knows Buzz can't fly. But that isn't important.

d Woody is Andy's favorite toy.

2 **Think about Woody in these scenes. Write Yes or No.**

I think he's ...	Yes	No	Yes	No
nice				
angry				
friendly				
happy				

Language

1 🎧 **Listen and read.**

2 **Read and write.**

1 John: .... you have a toy plane?

Amy: Yes, I ....

2 Sophia: Do .... like dolls?

Lucas: No, I ....

3 Dylan: .... your favorite toy?

Sarah: .... my brown bear.

4 Julia: .... you have a bicycle?

David: .... , I do.

3 **Practice the dialog. Use these words and your own.**

like   have   play with

toy elephants

toy buses

dolls

toy trucks

Phonics

1 🎧 **Listen and write the sound you hear: f or th.**

f ....

....

2 🎧 **Listen and write f or th.**

I ......ink I see a ......unny ......ace and ......ree ......in tee......

I ......ink I see a ......unny ......ace and ......our ......at tee......

3 🎧 **Read and circle. Listen and check.**

wife   with   thin   finish   mouth   mouse

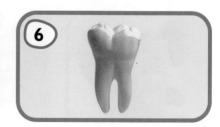

food   good   bad   bath   tooth   foot

Values: Self-belief

1 **Read and check.**

1 Woody and Buzz fly. Who makes it happen?

   a ◯ Woody   **b** ◯ Buzz   **c** ◯ Andy

2 How does he do that?

   a ◯ He uses a toy rocket.   **b** ◯ He uses his wings.

   c ◯ Andy's toys help him.

3 Who believes in his abilities?

   a ◯ Andy   **b** ◯ Woody   **c** ◯ Buzz

2 **Can you do something well? Draw and write.**

I can _____.

3 **Share.**

I can surf!

Find Out

1 **Look, read, and match.**

very old toys ....   old toys ....   toys today ....   new toys ....

 **Writing tip**

I like to play **with dolls.**
I want to play **with my new doll.**

Use a verb after **like to** and **want to**.

---

2 **Complete the sentences using *like to* or *want to*.**
Add a verb to sentences 4, 5 and 6.

1 .....I like to..... play games with my friends.

2 .... get a virtual reality toy
for my birthday.

3 .... give a teddy bear to my
baby sister.

4 .... things with blocks.

5 .... with my favorite toy.

6 .... pictures of animals.

Game Follow the Path

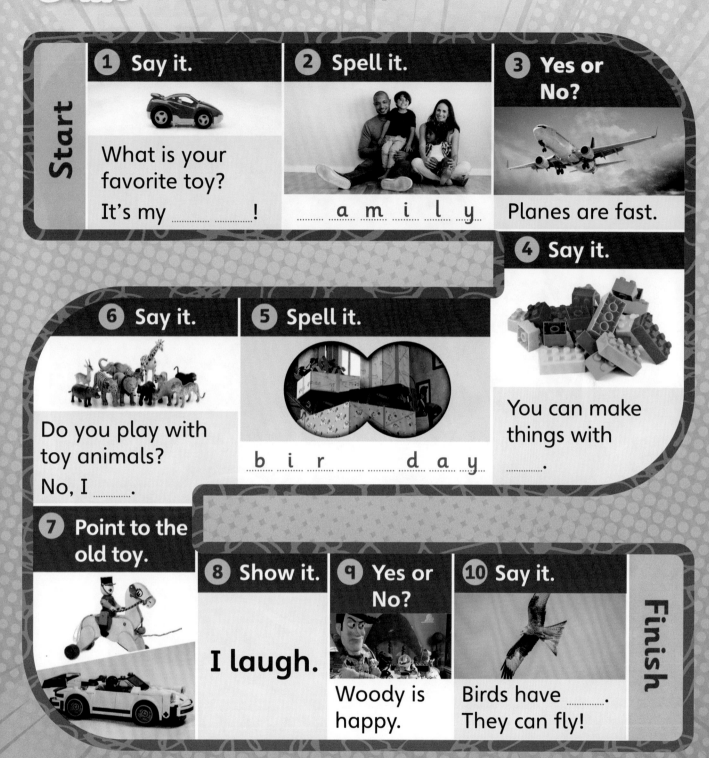

Start

① Say it.
What is your favorite toy?
It's my _____ _____!

② Spell it.
____ a m i l y

③ Yes or No?
Planes are fast.

④ Say it.
You can make things with _____.

⑤ Spell it.
b i r ____ d a y

⑥ Say it.
Do you play with toy animals?
No, I _____.

⑦ Point to the old toy.

⑧ Show it.
I laugh.

⑨ Yes or No?
Woody is happy.

⑩ Say it.
Birds have _____.
They can fly!

Finish

Now I can ...

○ name toys and their parts and say what they can do.

○ ask and say what things I like or have; name my favorite toy.

○ hear the difference between sounds for f and th and say them.

**What are the girls doing?
Look and say.**

Vocabulary

1 **Choose a or b.**

a freeze   **a** scared   **a** magic   **a** warm

b hold   **b** angry   **b** snowman   **b** weak

2 **Circle the odd one out.**

1 weak   scared   ice   **3** warm   cold   frozen

2 freeze   hit   melt   **4** angry   mountain   dangerous

3 **Look and write words from Activities 1 and 2. Find and draw the secret word.**

1 r a e d s c

2 y r n g a

3 o n t m a i u n

4 a m w r

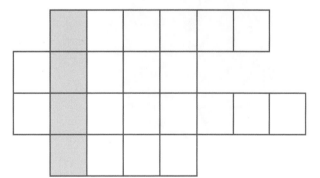

Story

1 **Answer the questions.**

1 Can Elsa make magic snow and ice?   Yes, she can.

2 Is Anna Queen of Arendelle?   ....

3 Does Elsa leave Arendelle?   ....

4 Does Kristoff want to help Anna?   ....

5 Does Elsa freeze?   ....

6 Does Elsa love her sister?   ....

2 **Choose scenes from the story. Write the page numbers.**

🙂   ☹   😮

(A happy scene)   (A sad scene)   (A scary scene)

page ....   page ....   page ....

Language

1 🎧 **Listen and read.**

2 **Match. What do you say?**

1 Nick's hands are dirty.

2 Marisa is hungry.

3 Vin's making noise .

4 Your bags are heavy.

5 The room is very hot.

6 Ben is bored.

"Play a computer game."

"Help me, please."

"Open the window, please."

"Be quiet, please."

"Wash your hands."

"Eat an apple."

3 **Practice the language. Use these words and your own.**

 I'm hungry.   Eat a banana.

hungry   thirsty   bored

banana   cake   egg   water   tea   juice   book   movie   picture

Phonics

1 🎧 **Listen and circle the correct letter. Then read.**

1  **s** **z** ock

2  **s** **z** ero

3  **s** **z** tore

4  qui **s** **z**

5  **s** **z** oo

6  bu **s** **z**

2 🎧 **Listen and write S, s, or z.**

A fro____en ____nowman is having fun,

Olaf ____ings, "I love the ____un!"

Free____ing bli____zards, ice and ____now,

____isters ____ing, "Let it go!"

3 🎧 **Read and match. Listen and check.**

(freeze)   (stop)   (sunny)   (zebra)   (mouse)

 1    2    3    4    5

Values: Responsibility

1 **Answer Yes or No.**

1

Elsa and Anna are playing. Elsa's ice hits Anna. Is Elsa sorry? ....

2

Elsa is angry. Her ice hits Anna. Is Elsa sorry?
....

2 **How about you? Do you say sorry for these things? Check (✔) or cross (✗).**

○ I eat my sister's chocolate.

○ I take my brother's things, but he doesn't know.

○ I play a game and I win.

○ I play loud music.

○ I sleep late on the weekend.

○ I am late for my lesson.

3 **Share.**

I say "I'm sorry" when I eat my sister's chocolate.

Find Out

1 **Read and choose a or b.**

1 The .... Festival is in Japan.

   a Ice   **b** Snow

2 They bring the snow with ....

   a planes   **b** trucks

3 They make .... with the snow.

   a sculptures   **b** mountains

4 At the end of the festival, ...

   a the snow melts   **b** they take the snow away

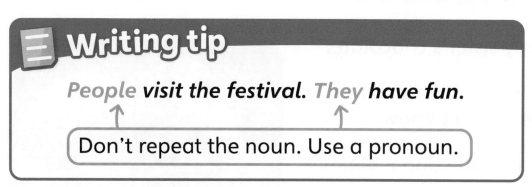

Writing tip

People **visit the festival.** *They* **have fun.**

Don't repeat the noun. Use a pronoun.

2 **Write the pronoun they, he or it.**

1 The snow arrives in trucks. .... is very clean and white.

2 People make sculptures with the snow. .... work carefully but quickly.

3 People enjoy the festival. .... buy hot drinks and food.

4 My brother goes to the festival every year. .... loves the snow slides.

Game Spin the Wheel

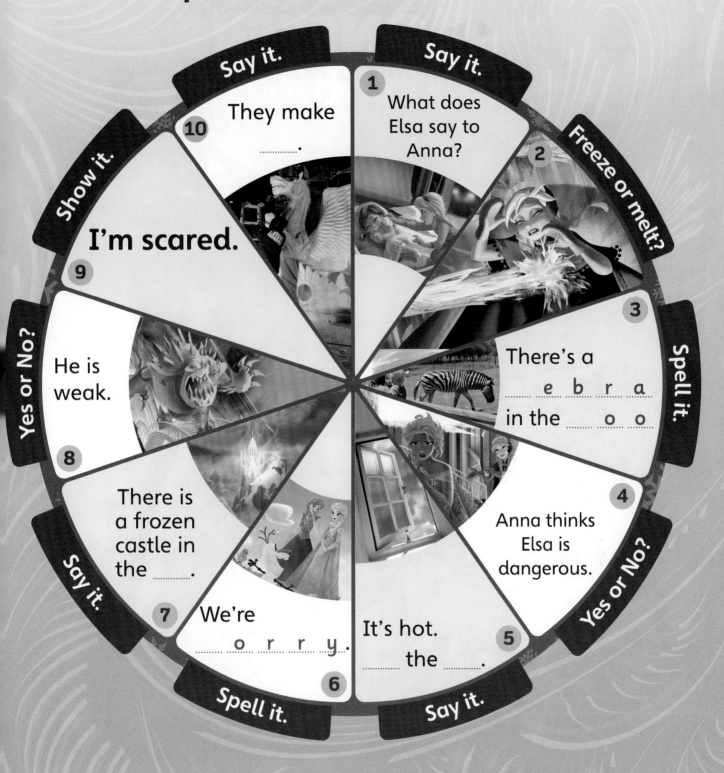

Say it.
10 They make
_____ .

Say it.
1 What does Elsa say to Anna?

Show it.
9 I'm scared.

Freeze or melt?
2

Yes or No?
8 He is weak.

Spell it.
3 There's a _____ e b r a in the _____ o o

Say it.
7 There is a frozen castle in the _____.

4 Anna thinks Elsa is dangerous.
Yes or No?

We're _____ o r r y.

It's hot. _____ the _____.

Spell it.
6

Say it.
5

Now I can...

○ name things and feelings connected to winter.

○ ask or tell people to do things.

○ hear the difference between the sounds for s and z and say them.

Book 6

Disney · PIXAR

MONSTERS UNIVERSITY

How many eyes do the monsters have? Point and say.

Vocabulary

1 **Choose and write.** team   university   fight   scare   monsters

1 Mike and Sulley are _____.

2 They go to _____. They are in the
   School of Scaring.

3 Sulley can _____ people. Mike can't.

4 Mike and Sulley are not friends. They _____.

5 They play in the Scare Games. They are on the same _____.

2 **Do the crossword.**

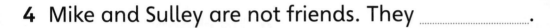
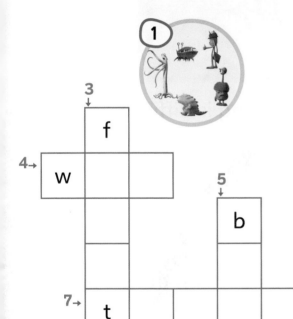
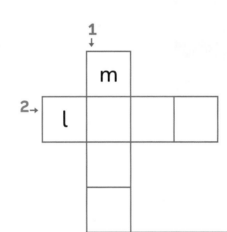

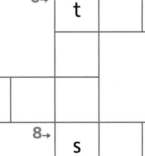

1 m
2→ l
3 f
4→ w
5 b
6→ t
7→ t
8→ s

Story

1 **Read and circle.**

1 Sulley is wrong.

   a He says "I'm sorry."

   b He says "No, I'm right!"

2 Mike wants to win.

   a He cheats.

   b He tries hard.

3 Oozma Kappa works as a team.

   a They're weak.

   b They're strong.

4 Scaring is difficult.

   a Mike works hard.

   b Mike stops.

2 **Draw and label your favorite monster from the story.**

This monster is ....
It has ....

Language

> ## 💬 Language
>
> **Can you** catch the ball?   **Can they** speak English?
> Yes, **I can**.   No, **they can't**.
> [ca**n't** = can**not**]

2 **Read and write.**

1 😊 Emily: .... your brother drive?

   😊 Mark: No, he ....

2 😊 Maya: Can .... draw a dog?

   😊 Owen: Yes, I .... It's easy!

3 😊 Eric: Can .... win this game?

   😊 Ruby: ...., they can't. It's difficult.

4 😊 Max: .... you and Jane work together?

   😊 Rachel: Yes, ...

3 **Practice the dialog. Use these words and your own.**

jump high

ride a horse

play basketball

run fast

45

Phonics

1 🎧 **Listen and draw lines to th or v.**

2 🎧 **Listen and write Th, th, or v.**

At _____is uni_____ersity, _____ey arri_____e and _____ey lea_____e,

A monster team is _____ere.   And _____ey make _____e children scared!

3 🎧 **Read the words. Check. Listen and check.**

	v (as in love)	th (as in **th**at)	f (as in **f**ast)	th (as in **th**ink)
1 movie	✔			
2 there				
3 foot				
4 mouth				
5 brother				
6 visit				

Values: Teamwork

1 Why do Oozma Kappa start winning games? Check.

They're strong and scary.   The games are easy.   They work together.

2 Check the things you like to do with other people. Add one more thing. Draw it.

○ play soccer/basketball

○ play computer games

○ clean my room

○ go for a walk

○ go on vacation

○ learn English

I _____

with _____.

3 Share.

I like to play soccer with my friends.

Find Out

1 Match the words (a–d) to the sentences (1–4).

a soccer

b baseball

1 You hit and catch the ball.

....

2 You kick the ball and run fast.

....

3 You play together.

....

c basketball

d team games

4 You throw and catch the ball.

....

Writing tip

You *don't* **kick the ball in basketball.**

He *doesn't* **play soccer.**

Use **don't** and **doesn't** to make negative statements.

2 Write the things you don't do in these games.

soccer

1 You .... (touch) the ball with your hands.

2 Players .... (kick) other players.

basketball

3 You .... (hit) the ball with a bat.

4 Players .... (wear) helmets.

baseball

5 The home team .... (start) the game.

6 You .... (kick) the ball with your feet.

Game Connect Three in a Line

1 What's the word?

n y i r u s v i e t

2 Spell it.

She's ___ e r ___ y scary.

3 Yes or No?

At the beginning, Mike and Sulley are friends.

4 Say it.

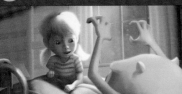

Can Mike scare a child?

___ he ___.

5 Hit or kick the ball?

6 Spell it.

The team works

t o g e ___ e r.

7 Say it.

In basketball, you play in a ___.

8 Say it.

___ ride a bicycle? Yes, I can!

9 Show it.

I win!

Now I can...

○ talk about playing different games.

○ ask and say what I can and can't do.

○ hear the difference between the sounds for th and v and say them.

1 🅐🅐 Read and check (✔) or cross (✗).

1 storm ⭕   **3** human ⭕   **5** mermaid ⭕

2 swim ⭕   **4** cloud ⭕   **6** ship ⭕

2 📖 Look, read, and circle.

1 Ariel is on **a ship** / **the beach**. She sees Prince Eric.

2 Prince Eric **falls in the water** / **is on the ship**. Ariel finds him.

3 Ariel wants to **sing** / **be human**. She loves Prince Eric.

4 King Triton is **happy** / **angry**. The prince is human.
She is a mermaid!

3 💬 Circle.

1 **Whose** / **Who's** shoes are these?
They're **Ethan** / **Ethan's** shoes.

2 Whose **bag** / **bags** is this?
It's **I** / **my** bag.

3 Whose books are **this** / **these**?
It's / **They're** Amal's books.

4 Whose fork **is** / **are** this?
It's **you** / **your** fork.

1  **Circle.**

1 reef / path

2 remember / forget

3 fish / shells

4 turtle / whale

5 octopus / stingray

6 tank / ocean

2 📖 **Read and circle.**

1 At the beginning of the story, **Dory gets lost / Dory's parents leave her**.

2 When Dory hits her head, she **remembers / forgets** her parents.

3 At the end of the story, Dory **brings her parents to meet her friends / forgets her friends**.

3 💬 **Write.**

1 What .... Mario doing?

.... is sleeping.

2 What are you ....?

I .... playing a computer game.

3 What .... your mom and dad doing?

They are .... TV.

1 🅐🅐 **Label the pictures.**

> snake   elephants   tiger   bear   monkeys   panther

1
....

2
....

3
....

4
....

5
....

6
....

2 📖 **Match.**

1 .... Mowgli has some friends in the jungle.

2 .... Shere Khan is dangerous. Mowgli is scared.

3 .... Mowgli meets Baloo. They have fun together.

4 .... Mowgli is not scared. He forgets Shere Khan!

a

b

c

d

3 💬 **Choose and write.**

> go   play   watch   sleep   do   what

1 What do you .... on the weekend?

I .... to the park with my friends.

2 .... do you do on the weekend?

We .... late. We .... TV. Then we .... games.

1 **Aa** **Read and match 1–4 to a–d.**

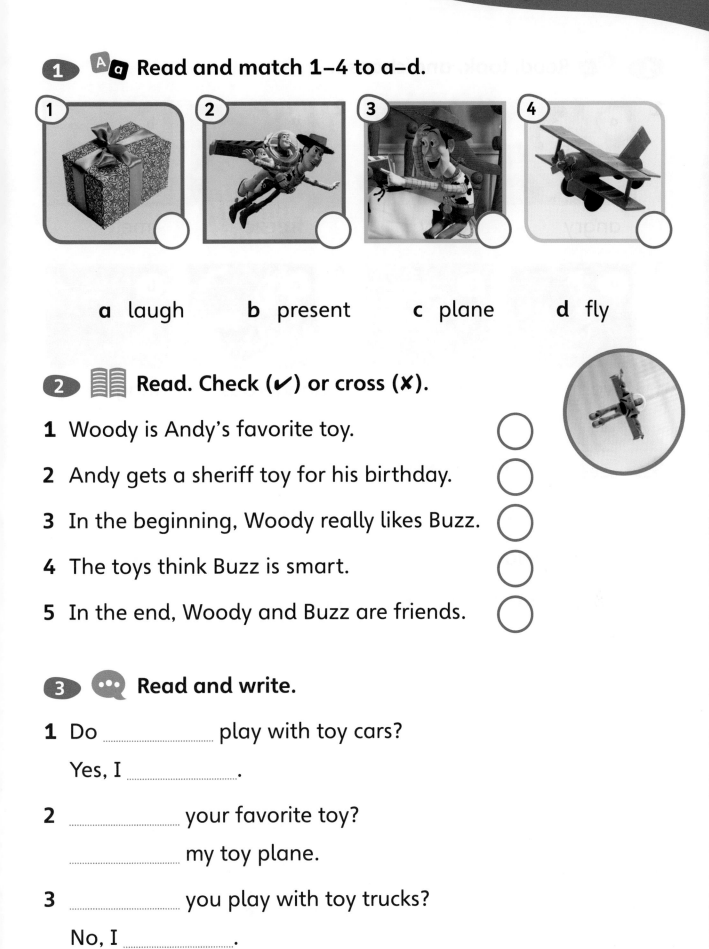

1

2

3

4

a laugh   **b** present   **c** plane   **d** fly

2 📖 **Read. Check (✔) or cross (✗).**

1 Woody is Andy's favorite toy.   ◯

2 Andy gets a sheriff toy for his birthday.   ◯

3 In the beginning, Woody really likes Buzz.   ◯

4 The toys think Buzz is smart.   ◯

5 In the end, Woody and Buzz are friends.   ◯

3 💬 **Read and write.**

1 Do _____ play with toy cars?

Yes, I _____.

2 _____ your favorite toy?

_____ my toy plane.

3 _____ you play with toy trucks?

No, I _____.

1 🅰🅰 Read, look, and choose.

1

angry _____   happy _____

2

freeze _____   melt _____

3

warm _____   scared _____

4

dangerous _____   magic _____

2 📖 Read. Check (✔) or cross (✗).

1 Elsa's magic snow and ice are dangerous.   ◯

2 Elsa runs away from Arendelle.   ◯

3 Elsa looks for Anna in the mountains.   ◯

4 A big snowman hits Anna. She is freezing.   ◯

5 Elsa is sorry. She loves her sister.   ◯

3 💬 Choose and write.

read   drink   walk   wear   eat   go

1 I'm hungry.   _____ some bread and cheese.

2 I'm thirsty.   _____ some water.

3 I'm tired.   _____ to bed, please.

4 I'm bored.   _____ a book.

1 **Look, read and write.**

1

i	n	w

4

s	r	a	y	c

2

a	e	m	t

5

r	a	b	e	k

3

t	g	h	i	f

6

l	e	o	s

2 **Correct the sentences.**

1 We work as a team—we are ~~weak~~.   strong

2 We want to win—we cheat.   ....

3 I'm wrong—I say nothing.   ....

4 This is difficult—I stop trying.   ....

3 **Write.**

1 .... you run fast?   ...., I can.

2 I .... jump high!   Wow!

3 Can .... catch the ball?   No, I ....

4 .... Andy speak English?   Yes, ... can.

Reading Record

Book 1
The Little Mermaid

This book: ☆ ☆ ☆ ☆ ☆

My favorite part:

Draw

My new words:

Write

STAMP

Book 2
Finding Dory

This book: ☆ ☆ ☆ ☆ ☆

My favorite part:

Draw

My new words:

Write

STAMP

Book 3
The Jungle Book

This book: ☆ ☆ ☆ ☆ ☆

My favorite part:

Draw

My new words:

Write

STAMP

Book 4
Toy Story

This book: ☆☆☆☆☆

My favorite part:

Draw

My new words:

Write

STAMP

Book 5
Frozen

This book: ☆☆☆☆☆

My favorite part:

Draw

My new words:

Write

STAMP

Book 6
Monsters University

This book: ☆☆☆☆☆

My favorite part:

Draw

My new words:

Write

STAMP

Spelling Practice

Look and say.	Look and write.	Cover and write.	✔
today			
here			
there			
this			
that			
these			
those			
What			
Where			
Who			
When			
Whose			
red			
blue			
yellow			
green			
black			
white			
brown			
gray			

Look and say.	Look and write.	Cover and write.	✔
don't			
doesn't			
aren't			
isn't			
can't			
look			
have			
play			
see			
like			
come			
live			
read			
eat			
buy			

Word List

a

about
all
angry
animal
answer
arm
arrive
ask
at
away

b

back
bad
badge
bag
ball
baseball
basketball
bath
beach
bear
beautiful
bed
bicycle
big
birthday
birthday party
blizzard
blocks

break
bring
book
bored
bug
bus
but
buy

c

cake
can
careful
carry
cat
catch
cheat
child
close
clothes
cloud
coconut
come
computer
game
cry
cut

d

dance
dangerous

dark
difficult
dirty
do
dog
doll
down
dream
drink
drive

e

easy
eat
elephant
end
eraser
every
excited

f

face
fall
far
fast
feet
festival
fight
find
fish
flower

fly
follow
foot
for
forget
fork
freeze
friendly
frozen
fruit
fun
funny

g

game
get
glasses
grandmother
great
go

h

hand
hard
hat
have fun
heart
heavy
help
her
hide

his
hit
hold
horse
hot
human

i

ice
idea
important
ink
interesting

j

jam
jeans
job
jug
juice
jump
jungle

k

kick
know

l

late
laugh
leave

leg
lightning
listen
live
long
look for
lose
loud
love

m

magic
make
man
mango
marbles
meet
melt
mermaid
milk
monkey
monster
mother
mountain
mouse
mouth
movies
music
my

n

new
night
noise
not
nut

o

octopus
of
okay
one
open
or
out of
over

p

panther
parent
park
party
path
pen
pencil
pet
place
plane
plant
play
point

pot
present
problem

q

quickly
quiet
quiz

r

rain
read
ready
red
reef
remember
river
ruler
run

s

sad
say
scare
scared
scary
school
sculpture
secret
see
shell
sheriff

ship
shoes
show
sing
sister
sit
size
ski
sleep
slow
small
smart
smile
snake
snow
snowman
soccer
sock
sorry
space ranger
squirt
stay
stingray
stop
store
storm
story
strong
suddenly
sunny

surf
swim

t

tail
take
talk
tall
tank
tea
team
teddy bear
teeth
tell
that
their
then
these
thing
think
this
thunder
tiger
time
tired
to
today
together
top
town
toy

train
tree
true
try
turtle

u

under
understand
university
up

v

vacation
vegetables
very
virtual reality
visit

w

wait
want
warm
wash
watch
way
weak
wear
weekend
well
whale
what

wheel
when
where
white
wife
win
windy
wing
with
woman
work

y

yard

z

zebra
zero
zoo